I'm In Business…!

The Ultimate Pun Joke Book

ISBN: 9798338313381
Cover art by Yasir Nadeem
With contributions from Jonny, Alex, Joe and Michael
First edition published September 2024

CONTENTS

HOW TO USE THIS BOOK

This book is best enjoyed with a friend. Setup the joke by reading the first line yourself, then have your partner answer with the first **bold statement.** You'll respond with the next line, and your partner will respond with the second **bold statement.** You can then hit them with the punchline and watch them groan.

The jokes are categorised into 3 chapters, with the jokes becoming progressively better or worse, you can decide.

—

We've added a few blank pages at the end of the book so you can have a go at creating your own. Once you've mastered these, try the bonus **reverse challenge,** found on the last 2 pages.

CHAPTER 1

MILD CRINGE

—

I'm in business…!

What business are you in?

I make steering wheels that only turn one way

How's it going for you?

It's all right

I'm in business…!

What business are you in?

I sell broken calculators

How's it going for you?

The numbers just aren't adding up

I'm in business…!

What business are you in?

I write horror novels in braille

How's it going for you?

Something bad is about to happen, I can just feel it

I'm in business…!

What business are you in?

I'm a garbage man

How's it going for you?

I'm picking it up as I go

I'm in business…!

What business are you in?

I'm a yoga instructor

How's it going for you?

The hours are pretty flexible

I'm in business…!

What business are you in?

I have my own range of bespoke

scarecrows

How's it going for you?

They're not just great, they're outstanding

in their field

I'm in business…!

What business are you in?

I make mirrors that never stay clean

How's it going for you?

I can't see myself in it for long

I'm in business…!

What business are you in?

I make fairground attractions based on Mexican food

How's it going for you?

The guac-a-mole has gone down a storm

I'm in business…!

What business are you in?

I run a retirement home for elderly twins

How's it going for you?

Well you know... same old, same old

I'm in business…!

What business are you in?

I'm an unsuccessful doctor who easily

becomes annoyed

How's it going for you?

I've got absolutely no patients

I'm in business…!

What business are you in?

I eat watches

How's it going for you?

It's time consuming

I'm in business…!

What business are you in?

I juice depressed fruits then carbonate them

How's it going for you?

It's soda pressing

I'm in business…!

What business are you in?

I manufacture elevators

How's it going for you?

It has its ups and downs

I'm in business…!

What business are you in?

I run a successful chain of prison libraries

How's it going for you?

It has its prose and cons

I'm in business…!

What business are you in?

I make calendars that you can turn into

paper aeroplanes

How's it going for you?

The days keep on flying by

I'm in business…!

What business are you in?

I dig attractive holes in the ground

How's it going for you?

Pretty well

I'm in business…!

What business are you in?

I rent out chef whites

How's it going for you?

My overall performance is pretty good

I'm in business…!

What business are you in?

I recycle old footwear

How's it going for you?

It's sole destroying

I'm in business…!

What business are you in?

I run a facility for people who can't make their minds up

How's it going for you?

I'm not sure

I'm in business…!

What business are you in?

I sell pre-tied lengths of rope

How's it going for you?

It's knot for me

I'm in business…!

What business are you in?

I work in the escape room business

How's it going for you?

I want out

I'm in business…!

What business are you in?

I manufacture wheelchairs

How's it going for you?

I can't stand it

I'm in business…!

What business are you in?

I sell yachts that are powered by the wind

How's it going for you?

Well, sails are up

I'm in business…!

What business are you in?

I work in the demolition business

How's it going for you?

Booming

I'm in business…!

What business are you in?

I get paid to pull up roots with my bare hands

How's it going for you?

I'm not digging it

I'm in business…!

What business are you in?

I help people fulfil their lifelong dream of becoming a human cannonball

How's it going for you?

Not great - I just got fired

I'm in business…!

What business are you in?

I own several libraries

How's it going for you?

Business is pretty quiet

I'm in business…!

What business are you in?

I'm a parking enforcer

How's it going for you?

Fine

I'm in business…!

What business are you in?

I make vacuum cleaners

How's it going for you?

It sucks

I'm in business…!

What business are you in?

I create religious statues

How's it going for you?

I'm yet to make a prophet

I'm in business…!

What business are you in?

I run a company that specialises in weighing tiny objects

How's it going for you?

It's a small scale operation

I'm in business…!

What business are you in?

I make boats in my attic

How's it going for you?

Sales are through the roof

I'm in business…!

What business are you in?

I work in banking

How's it going for you?

I've lost interest

I'm in business…!

What business are you in?

I'm in the origami business

How's it going for you?

We've just folded

I'm in business…!

What business are you in?

I train lifeguards

How's it going for you?

Swimmingly

I'm in business…!

What business are you in?

I lay gravel at the beginning of races

How's it going for you?

We were off to a rocky start

I'm in business…!

What business are you in?

I lead a team of people who are trying to break into virtual bank vaults

How's it going for you?

I'm not sure I can hack it

I'm in business…!

What business are you in?

I sell mood rings

How's it going for you?

I'm not sure how I feel about it

I'm in business…!

What business are you in?

I make reversible jackets

How's it going for you?

I'm excited to see how it turns out

I'm in business…!

What business are you in?

I sell whiteboards

How's it going for you?

Re-markable

I'm in business…!

What business are you in?

I sell equipment for wizards

How's it going for you?

I just can't get the staff

I'm in business…!

What business are you in?

I built an app that teaches people sign language

How's it going for you?

It's pretty handy

I'm in business…!

What business are you in?

I sell blunt pencils

How's it going for you?

Pointless

I'm in business…!

What business are you in?

I sell hand-held fans

How's it going for you?

It blows

I'm in business…!

What business are you in?

I'm writing a book about anti-gravity

How's it going for you?

It's impossible to put down

I'm in business…!

What business are you in?

I sell magnets that have two north poles

How's it going for you?

It's hard to make ends meet

I'm in business…!

What business are you in?

I sell broken helicopters

How's it going for you?

I'm not sure it'll take off

I'm in business…!

What business are you in?

I write novels that never reach a

conclusion

How's it going for you?

I'm losing the plot

I'm in business…!

What business are you in?

I send people into space

How's it going for you?

It's out of this world

I'm in business…!

What business are you in?

I breed horses

How's it going for you?

Business is stable

I'm in business…!

What business are you in?

I fix clock tower roofs

How's it going for you?

I'm always working over time

I'm in business…!

What business are you in?

I create belts that are made out of watches

How's it going for you?

It's a waist of time

I'm in business…!

What business are you in?

I'm a funeral director

How's it going for you?

I only work mournings

I'm in business…!

What business are you in?

I run a repair shop for small, broken
violins

How's it going for you?

The work is very fiddly

I'm in business…!

What business are you in?

I make miniature notebooks

How's it going for you?

There's not much margin in it

I'm in business…!

What business are you in?

I'm a professional dog walker

How's it going for you?

It's a walk in the park

I'm in business…!

What business are you in?

I've recently started a lawn care company

How's it going for you?

I don't think I can cut it

I'm in business…!

What business are you in?

I sell cranes to the construction industry

How's it going for you?

Business is picking up

I'm in business…!

What business are you in?

I sell legal marijuana

How's it going for you?

Sales are at an all time high

I'm in business…!

What business are you in?

I'm in the hotel business

How's it going for you?

I fear a hostel takeover

I'm in business…!

What business are you in?

I drill holes all day

How's it going for you?

It's boring

I'm in business…!

What business are you in?

I run a dress alterations business

How's it going for you?

Sew sew

I'm in business…!

What business are you in?

I run an amusement park

How's it going for you?

Fair

I'm in business...!

What business are you in?

I manufacture submarines

How's it going for you?

We just went under

I'm in business…!

What business are you in?

I run a cemetery

How's it going for you?

People are dying to get in

I'm in business…!

What business are you in?

I design ultramarathon courses

How's it going for you?

I'm in it for the long run

CHAPTER 2

MEDIUM CRINGE

—

I'm in business…!

What business are you in?

I've recently become the dictator of a
small Asian nation

How's it going for you?

It's fine for now but I don't think I can
make a Korea out of it

I'm in business…!

What business are you in?

I run an 90s British R&B themed Apple
Store

How's it going for you?

I've been having a few issues with the
return of the macs

I'm in business…!

What business are you in?

I'm a cheesemonger who makes headwear
for horses

How's it going for you?

Not great - it turns out it's very difficult to
mascarpone

I'm in business…!

What business are you in?

I run a music festival where the stages are
made of cheese

How's it going for you?

I have only one in the portfolio so far;
Glaston-brie

I'm in business…!

What business are you in?

I run a sausage factory that's in constant competition with the Germans

How's it going for you?

I'm always fearing the wurst

I'm in business…!

What business are you in?

I recycle discarded chewing gum

How's it going for you?

I'm really struggling to get it off the
ground

I'm in business…!

What business are you in?

I run a chain of Mexican restaurants

How's it going for you?

It doesn't peso well

I'm in business…!

What business are you in?

I own a large number of factories, all

producing orange juice

How's it going for you?

There's so much going on, it's hard to

concentrate

I'm in business…!

What business are you in?

I sell trampolines in Prague

How's it going for you?

We're getting a lot of orders, but the
Czechs keep on bouncing

I'm in business…!

What business are you in?

I run a support group for blackjack dealers
with itchy feet

How's it going for you?

I think I can get a better deal elsewhere

I'm in business…!

What business are you in?

I run an acupuncture clinic with my ex-partner

How's it going for you?

I often feel like I've been stabbed in the back

I'm in business…!

What business are you in?

I run a support group for people who like

to talk about an object's matter

How's it going for you?

Solid

I'm in business…!

What business are you in?

I manage a team of hurdlers who have

never lost a race

How's it going for you?

We're strides ahead of the competition

I'm in business…!

What business are you in?

I run an axe-throwing business for people
with poor aim

How's it going for you?

We rarely hit our targets

I'm in business…!

What business are you in?

I'm a doctor specialising in prostate examinations

How's it going for you?

It's a pain in the ass

I'm in business…!

What business are you in?

I travel around the country giving seminars on the benefits of eating dried grapes

How's it going for you?

I'm raisin awareness

I'm in business…!

What business are you in?

I make period dramas

How's it going for you?

Everyone keeps overy-acting

I'm in business…!

What business are you in?

I'm a trainee hangman

How's it going for you?

Right now they're just showing me the

ropes

I'm in business…!

What business are you in?

I dig for precious stones

How's it going for you?

We've been having some miner difficulties

I'm in business…!

What business are you in?

I'm in the inauguration business

How's it going for you?

I've been Biden my time for about 4 years

now

CHAPTER 3

SEVERE CRINGE

—

I'm in business…!

What business are you in?

I work at Ikea

How's it going for you?

It's great, I get to take a lot of Stockholm

I'm in business…!

What business are you in?

I advise Craig David on his archery equipment

How's it going for you?

You could say I'm his Bo Selector

I'm in business…!

What business are you in?

I've recently started working at Old
MacDonald's Farm

How's it going for you?

Well, I'm hoping to become the CIEIO

I'm in business…!

What business are you in?

I help one-armed typists

How's it going for you?

It's mostly shift work

I'm in business…!

What business are you in?

I create oversized statues of women, made

out of meat

How's it going for you?

I've made a huge Miss Steak

I'm in business…!

What business are you in?

I build software that simulates horse-drawn carriages

How's it going for you?

The first release was a little buggy

I'm in business…!

What business are you in?

I'm re-designing the green man in traffic lights

How's it going for you?

It's making me cross

I'm in business…!

What business are you in?

I run an emigration business, trying to convince people to move to Switzerland

How's it going for you?

Well, the flag is a big plus

I'm in business…!

What business are you in?

I export artificial limbs to hospitals in

foreign countries

How's it going for you?

It's pretty tough being an international

arms dealer

I'm in business…!

What business are you in?

I sell recycled shoes that used to belong to
drug dealers

How's it going for you?

I'm not sure what they'd been laced with
but I'm always tripping

I'm in business…!

What business are you in?

I run a Vietnamese restaurant but I'm under investigation for treating my staff badly

How's it going for you?

The government are trying to banh mi from the area

I'm in business…!

What business are you in?

I run a food bank that specialises in giving

out small vegetables

How's it going for you?

It's difficult. I recently had to turn

somebody away because they had taken too

many onions. I said "that's shallot"

I'm in business…!

What business are you in?

I remake childhood stories where the main character is tripping on acid

How's it going for you?

We've just released Jack and the Beans Talk

I'm in business…!

What business are you in?

I run a theatre that showcases Shakespeare plays using a cast consisting entirely of pencils

How's it going for you?

It's early days still… I can't work out whether it's 2B or not 2B

That's it, we're all joke'd out. That was 100 cringeworthy jokes that we hope had you grinning from ear to ear.

The next 10 pages contain just the **setup statements**, so you can come up with your own jokes.

I'm in business…!

What business are you in?

How's it going for you?

I'm in business...!

What business are you in?

How's it going for you?

I'm in business…!

What business are you in?

How's it going for you?

I'm in business...!

What business are you in?

How's it going for you?

I'm in business…!

What business are you in?

How's it going for you?

I'm in business…!

What business are you in?

How's it going for you?

I'm in business…!

What business are you in?

How's it going for you?

I'm in business…!

What business are you in?

How's it going for you?

I'm in business…!

What business are you in?

How's it going for you?

I'm in business…!

What business are you in?

How's it going for you?

—

Up next, a bonus challenge.

BONUS: REVERSE CHALLENGE

Here are some punchlines that you can give to a friend and have them **reverse engineer** the joke, coming up with a hilarious setup.

I'm just trying to get a foot in the door

It doesn't work

How's what going for me?

The pay isn't great but the tips are enormous

Well.. all your business is under the table

Swings and roundabouts

Egg-cellent

I'd love to tell you but affogato

I thought I'd lost my job but my boss said I could wipe

the slate clean

It didn't workout for me

Pants

I didn't try hard enough

Grate

It's very testing

Every day is different

We're like a family

It's not very practical

We rarely win anything

I don't have a clue

Finances are fluid

Our stocks have recently taken a hit

Thrilling

It didn't last long

The business was accidental

Ask me in another time

We had to delay our launch

Printed in Dunstable, United Kingdom